MW00772389

B Christen

To a lovely soul
continue to impact lives
and be a blessing to all.

Much Love

TRUE SUCCESS

THE BLUEPRINT

CREATING THE LIFE

WANT STARTS WITH
THE BLUEPRINT

THURLESTER ROBINSON, JR.

© 2020 by Thurlester Robinson

All rights reserved. No part of this book may be used or reproduced in any manner whatsoever without written permission except in the case of brief quotations embodied in critical articles or reviews.

ISBN 978-1-09830-665-6

IN LOVING MEMORY OF

Thurlester Robinson, Sr.

Joyce Lamar

Andy Gobczynski

ACKNOWLEDMENT

My Legacy:

Aaryn Robinson

Thurlester Robinson III

Anthony Thurlester Robinson

Kennedy Thurlester Robinson

Cheyanne Robinson

My Siblings

Anthony Lamar

Rodney Lamar

Marlania Lamar

Nicola Lamar

Latoya Lamar Bady

Koron Lamar

Alem Lamar

(My Life) support system in alphabetical order:

Berry Bryant

Dorie Davis

Raymond Dozier

Sharon Dozier

Sam Dozier

Kelvin Hamner

Haywood Hunt

Denise Hollinshed

David Jones

Big Da Keys

Kris Keys

Carolyn Keys

Tony Keys

Louis Neil

Calvin Nelson

Jessie Page

Daryl Page

Erika Robinson

Patricia Tatum

Melvin Tatum

Jesse Taylor

Shane Williamson

Also, to all my nieces, nephews, friends and family members
unnamed I love you and appreciate you.

Contents

Contents

FORWARD

A Positive Attitude Leads to Success

I remember when I was 14, my friend and I decided we were going to be professional Basketball players. One day we were practicing dribbling around the neighborhood, and a car pulled upon us and a guy popped out of the sunroof and started shooting at us. We both bolted in the same direction towards the creek. We ran, we leaped over fences, cut though yards, and continued to run for what seemed like forever. We finally made our way to his house and he cried for what felt like hours. When he finally calmed down, he said that he would never play basketball again. I told him how lucky we were that we did not get hit and that had we not been in such great condition from working out for basketball, then we may have been shot. Every situation in life has two viewpoints, a positive one and a negative one, you have the option to choose, do so wisely.

INTRODUCTION

My humble beginnings shaped who I am today.

My name, Thurlester Robinson Jr., originated from my grandmother, Rosie Robinson. She named my father, Thurlester Robinson, Sr, after her favorite two uncles -Thurman and Lester. My origin is St. Louis, Missouri, and I am one of eight siblings. I have three brothers and four sisters, but only two of us share my Dad.

In the beginning, I lived happily with my mom, Dad, and four siblings. We resided in a lovely suburb of St. Louis called University City. My mom, Joyce, was a homemaker. Although she had very little education, she was extremely bright and resourceful. She got pregnant in seventh grade and became a wife at the age of fifteen. Becoming a wife and mother at an early age was not unusual for her family. Her mom and her grandmom had kids around the same age. Joyce divorced her husband and took custody of her three children. She met my Dad immediately after her divorce. Love at first sight is how she recalled it. Shortly after she started dating my Dad, she found out she had stage four stomach cancer. The doctors told my Dad to make funeral arrangements and prepare for my mom to die. Miraculously, she survived and beat the disease. She had no plans of having more kids because the doctors told her it would not be physically possible. Once again, she defied all odds and medical assertions by miraculously having more children. Two of the children by my Dad, Thurlester Robinson, Sr.

My Dad, Thurlester Robinson, Sr., finished high school and went to Forest Park Community College to pursue a business degree. While in college he worked two full time jobs to pay for school. Then he met my mom and decided that he would finish school later to help her take care of her three kids. My dad was very proud and old fashion because he believed his women should not work. He was an excellent provider, so mom never worked. We lived in a three-bedroom apartment comfortably. I remember my parents' big California king bed in their room, which I later learned was our living room. Mom told me that even though my Dad made a ton of money working multiple jobs, he lived very humble to save money for the kids to go to college. Dad was very good with money. He taught all of us the importance of making money and making good decisions with your money. He was a mentor to many and the go-to man in the community when there was a problem. He prided himself on taking care of family as well as teaching, mentoring, and taking care of his friends.

According to my mom and siblings, Thurlester Sr. was an amazing father, a great husband, and a caring friend. My mom told me that he was always the happiest person in the room. My siblings and I can attest to that. He was extremely playful and happy. He made it a point to teach us how to be confident, productive, and independent. Everyone loved him and depended on him. He was always helping people out financially or counseling them out of bad situations. He was very big on family. I recall spending lots of time with him daily. We worked out on a regular basis and he taught me how to count and earn money. He always allowed me to earn money by doing small tasks for him. He also encouraged me to charge family members when they needed me to do something. By the time I was five, I had a job delivering telephone books. I remember so clearly pulling up to different locations in my Dad's big black Fleetwood Cadillac and putting the telephone books on people's doorsteps.

My Dad made it very clear that making money and exercising was an essential part of life. We were a very healthy and fit family. He did not drink alcohol nor entertain any type of drugs. Dad was very big on leading by example. I recall doing so many fun family activities. Mom confirmed that Dad made it a major priority of his to spend as much time with family as he could. We had so many picnics and family outings at Forest Park that I thought he owned it. I had the perfect life.

July 4, 1982, my life took a turn in the opposite direction. Almost instantly it went from awesome and amazing to horrible. It started like any other Fourth of July holiday. My dad and I would go to the meat market on Grand Blvd. to get meat for the family B.B.Q. I recall going to the market that morning with him on his back, which was my usual means of traveling everywhere. Instead of making me get off his shoulders to go into the store, he ducked under the doorway. He carried me through the store and up through the checkout line. Staying on his shoulders was a little unusual because I typically had to get down when we enter somewhere. I recall checking out and him getting change for a dollar and handing me four quarters. I gladly accepted, but thought it was a little weird because I always had to work or complete some type of task to earn money.

That evening I recall my dad tucking me into bed, not with a book, which was our norm, but with an actual story that he made up. I do not recall exactly all the words, but I remember his point was to never settle for being broke and that no one ever truly dies because everyone will return during the resurrection. A few hours later, I was awakened by screams and outcries of my mom and aunt. I walked to the doorway of the bedroom, and my favorite auntie quickly turned me around and comforted me back to sleep. When I got up the next morning, I learned my dad died that night in his sleep. He had hypertension (high blood pressure) and was not aware of it. Although he lived a very healthy lifestyle with no alcohol or drugs and lots of exercises, his condition was hereditary. My mom said that he woke up during the middle of the night and told her he had a dream that he died. He returned to bed and passed away shortly afterward. Two months following the tragic loss of my dad, my favorite auntie was murdered.

3

In my eyes, Thurlester Robinson Sr. exemplified the meaning of true success through his attitude, actions, and lifestyle. He was doing exactly what he wanted and loved to do every day with the people he loved. He was admired and looked up to not only from his family, but by everyone with whom he came in contact.

Since age 6, I always wanted to be like my Dad. Although he was only in my life for six short years before he passed, he made a considerable impression on me. Everything I could remember and anything that everyone told me about him, I have tried to follow. Everyone I talked to about him said he was very generous, and there was never a problem that he could not solve. His positive attitude, friendly nature, and problem-solving mindset have been a few of my target objectives.

To date, I have been the cure to many challenging situations for friends, family, and co-workers. I make it a point to go out of my way to help anyone that I can. For many years I have been sharing, educating, and mentoring what I know about real estate, fitness, education, finances, and many other topics that have been an interest or concern to help others. I have been teaching what I have learned throughout life experiences from successes as well as failures.

Motivating and assisting people to accomplish goals is a passion of mine. This is what makes being a teacher so rewarding for me. Although teaching accounts for a small portion of my income, it's one of the most satisfying. My most heartfelt goal is to be able to make a positive difference in someone's life. My goal in education is to not only teach but to mentor, model, and care for my students. I aim to do the same for parents, co-workers, and all I encounter.

Thanks to my positive attitude growing up, I was able to make it through my challenging childhood after my Dad passed away. There was a long series of unfortunate circumstances that impacted everyone in my family. The next cycle of my life was a dysfunctional disaster by any and all standards of living.

Following the untimely death of Thurlester Robinson, Sr., the wholesome family dynamic we once knew instantly shattered. My mom moved us from our lovely apartment to a rat-infested building. I am sure the apartment building was condemned or at least should have been. We were only there for a year, but it felt like eternity. I can still hear the snaps of the rats getting caught in the traps. Eventually my mom grief turned her to drugs for comfort. I remember not seeing or hearing from her for days at a time. My siblings were majorly impacted as well. One sibling was slipped some laced marijuana, which resulted in him becoming schizophrenic. Another sibling started making bad decisions and was in and out of jail for long periods of time. Everyone seemed to have turned to something negative to help comfort Dad passing.

The only way I survived this ordeal was by relying on the mental toughness my father taught me. It was imperative that I change the narrative on every negative experience that presented itself to me. I always figured a way to make it favorable or at least reflect on something positive from it.

Once my Dad's life insurance money arrived, my mom purchased a house in North County. In the early '80s, North County, St. Louis, was a nice family-friendly oriented place to live. I quickly learned that was not true for all North County, especially my neighborhood. Just when I figured that things would be better, they got worse. Crips, Bloods, and Crack had just got introduced to my neighborhood, Sun Valley. Majority of the people in my community were involved in the gang and or drug infestation. I don't know who I was most afraid of, the gang members or the crack addicts. Both groups were very dangerous and unpredictable, and made going outside my home extremely dangerous and complicated. I can recall actually walking through forest like greenery and crossing a creek just to go to the corner store, because the street route was not safe.

Inside my home was not much safer. My brother's schizophrenia had led him to become violent, and most of the time I was at home alone with him. On top of that, the even more frightening issue was I had to share a room with him. Any time my mom was home, I had to sleep in the bedroom with him. I would wait for him to leave the room and quickly sneak under my bed to sleep. Anytime I had to use the bathroom I would be too scared to move, so I would just use it on myself. I was so afraid to move that a few times I did "number 2" on myself.

By the time I was about 9, it became so dangerous to be around him that most of the time I would just stay in this inoperable car parked under our carport. I had no adult supervision at this point. Daily, I had to figure out how to stay safe at home and how to eat. My siblings were scrambled about figuring out how to take care of themselves and survive as well. In order to eat I had to figure out how to make some money. At my age I could not get a job and it was challenging trying to find work in my environment. I started begging on the streets for money. I remember many days on the corner of Halls Ferry and Lucas Hunt with my empty milk jug container that read, "Collecting Money for Multiple Sclerosis". For a while, this earned me enough money to eat. Days when this was not successful I had to figure out an alternative means to eat. So, I started stealing. I would go to the Food for Less grocery store and steal lunchmeat. This was the easiest item to steal because the package was small. Another attractive component was I could eat it without any preparation. Every day I set two important goals for myself, eat and survive. This was my only focus. Going to school was safe and I could get a few free meals. That was all the motivation I needed to get good grades and not get in trouble.

As winter rolled around, it became harder for me to make money begging. Lucky or unlucky for me, my sister started dating a criminal. This individual started involving me in his criminal activity. He forced me to participate in his burglary business, aka breaking in homes. I labeled it his burglary business because this was his primary source of income. He burglarized homes almost daily. He would dress nicely and leave the house every day in the early morning and return in the evenings with all types of expensive items. When he forced me to go, my job was to knock on the front door to see if anyone was home. I always had a box of candy bars in case someone answered. On occasions when people answered, I would tell them that I am raising money for my basketball team. If no one answered, then he would break in the home through the front door with a crowbar, or I would climb through an open window. Once we were in, he would only steal things of value that he could sell. Sometimes we would burglarize houses of people he knew and called his friends. No matter how much we made, my share was always the same; I earned five dollars and a order of plain fried rice from my favorite Chinese restaurant. I could always tell when it was a good heist because he would add meat to my rice.

The most terrifying burglary we did was the last one for me. I will never forget the betrayal and the fear I felt. We left bright and early in the morning, as we would always do. I knocked on the door, and there was no answer. He broke the lock with the crowbar, and we entered the home. The first thing I did was to go into the kitchen and look in the refrigerator for food-that was always my first stop. I noticed a police utility belt on the table. I run upstairs to tell him that we are in a police officer's house. He told me not to worry and to hurry up and check the bedrooms. While we are rummaging through the house looking for valuables, the officer came home. I saw a squad car pull in the driveway, and I run upstairs again to alert the "master mind" of the business. Without hesitation, he jumped out a two-story window and left me behind. I quickly exited through the back door and ran as fast as I could through the alley. I heard tires burning rubber and sirens almost instantly. I jumped in a dumpster and closed the lid. I stayed in that dumpster at least ten hours. When I finally peaked out, it was nighttime. I wandered around for hours, trying to make it home. I had no money, and even if I had a dime to make a call, we never had a working phone at home, so there was no one I could have contacted to help me out. Accustomed to being in sticky situations, I walked for hours until I saw a street sign that was familiar. I somehow made it home by dawn the next day. There was no one looking for me, and no one even noticed that I was missing. At that point, I made the decision that I was not going to ever to allow him or anyone to make me burglarize homes again.

Ironically, he got caught soon after that incident and was sentenced to 10 years in prison. Lucky for me, I started selling candy bars at school. I quickly realized that this was an excellent idea because everyone wanted candy at school, and there was no one to get it from. Selling candy taught me a lot about supply, demand, and building relationships. The candy business was my first successful business venture. I saved up enough money to purchase me a car at age 12.

Finally, I was mobile and could do a lot more. Around this time, gangs and drugs like crack cocaine and weed where visible to my city and my neighborhood embraced it. Unfortunately, so did my family. Not so much the gang drama, but the crack and weed were a huge problem. The epidemic truly hit home. Most of my family dealt with the drug in some fashion. My mom still mourning my Dad's passing, became a victim of a highly addictive drug.

I observed a lot of negative situations and occasions pertaining to the drugs. As a young kid, I was exposed to drugs being cooked, used, bought, and sold. I paid close attention to the effects that it had on everyone around me. It was then that I made my mine up that I would never allow any of this to be a part of my life.

My neighborhood became a drug and gang-infested war zone. We were in North County, St. Louis, which back then was supposed to be considered a nice, safe suburb, but it was not the case for my subdivision. One positive thing for me during this time was that everyone who sold drugs and hung out on the corners loved candy and snacks. So, I was able to expand my candy business to chips and other snacks. In my car I had a corner store number of snacks to sell. I changed my entire image from Thurlester, the piss pot boy to the Candyman of the Junior High School and my neighborhood.

I upgraded my living conditions from the car to a pretty well-built tent / house type structure in the back yard. My Godmother

Sharon, found out where I was sleeping daily and allowed me to move in. She had always been a guardian angel of mine. She was my best friend, Raymond's mom. Ms. Sharon took me in as if I was her own. She was a single mom already raising her two sons, and she gladly took me in as her 3rd son. It was a pleasant change of lifestyle. I called Sharon mom. Every day, mom cooked breakfast and dinner. She worked long hours at the Wonder-Bread factory, but that never stopped her from having food on the table or in the fridge. It was amazing to come home to cooked food. I was living the dream with the necessities most people take for granted. I had my own room, hot water for baths, lights, heat, and a telephone. It seemed surreal. It gave me a clear understanding of what the good life felt like. For most people, it would be considered standard, but for me and for how I lived the previous six years, this was heaven.

My teenage years with mommy Sharon were terrific. She never knew that I made good money selling snacks and doing odd jobs because she gave me a weekly allowance. My best friend, Raymond, whom I consider a brother, knew that I made good money doing odd jobs, so sometimes he would come with me when he wanted to make some money.

Raymond was a great role model for me. He was athletic, smart, and a women magnet. So, I followed a lot in his footsteps with those traits, or at least I tried. I looked up to him, although I was about a foot taller. Ray played football, so I played football. I did not like wearing the helmet and the tights, so that did not last long. Ray played basketball, so I played basketball. Now, this was more like it.

I fell in love with basketball the first time I played. My older best friend, who I consider to be another big brother from another mother, was Louis. He was my godsent mentor who taught me a lot of basketball. Louis was a few years older than me and had the wisdom of a monk and the basketball game of a professional. The only thing that held him back was his height, but he was a fantastic football player as well. I credit him with my jump shot and handles.

Louis, Raymond, and I all shared the same views on not drinking alcohol or entertaining any drugs, although everyone around us did. I learned how to exist in a structured setting and how to be part of a functional family. A lot of negative things that was going on with my biological family, I had to block out in order to pursue my dreams. Over the years, I decided that where I come from does not determine where I am heading. Around 18, my senior year of high school, the social security check for me that my mom had been receiving since my dad passed came in my name. My mom wanted me to sign my checks over to her, and because I would not, she raised a lot of problems with mommy Sharon for allowing me to live with her. So, I moved out and got my own apartment.

Raymond went to college at the local community college and he encouraged me to do the same. I knew nothing about college except that rich people went there. I never thought that I would be able to afford to go to college, but Raymond helped me get a basketball scholarship to Forest Park Community College. He also introduced me to my other big brother from another Mother, Tony. Tony was a few years older than me and played basketball at the community college. Tony and I clicked instantly, and we resembled each other. He was basically my twin brother born from a different mother. Tony mentored me to the next step of becoming a scholar star athlete like he was. His parents treated me like a son instantly. Even his little brother Kris acknowledged me as his other big brother.

My second year of college I grew 6 inches, which took me from average player to all-star. I received a lot of division one scholarship offers and many college coaches contacted me. All the coaches wanted to meet my parents. I knew nothing about this star athlete life, but Tony walked me through it. I had Tony's parents who I refer to as mommy Keys and big DA, meet with the different college coaches as my parents. It was such an amazing experience being flown out and treated like a king by different universities who were trying to persuade me to come play for them. There are so many experiences I can't mention, just understand for a poor black kid that grew up in the hood this was heaven. I was starting to understand how important life decisions and timing were. After numerous official and unofficial visits to universities, I came together with Mom, Tony and Big DA and we decided that I should go to Mercer University. I wanted to major in criminal justice and then go to Law School, so Mercer was the perfect fit.

Leaving Saint Louis, Missouri, was super easy. I did not know what the world had to offer, but I was sure it was going to be better than home. Part of my signing with Mercer, I negotiated that I wanted to move to Georgia as soon as I graduated from Forest Park Community College.

I graduated May 12 and was on the highway May 13, headed to Georgia. I had never been out of Saint Louis alone, and I did not know how to read a map. I had a 1982 Ford Crown Victoria, all my clothes packed in two trash bags and about 300 bucks. My coach gave me directions, and I wrote it down on a brown paper bag that I got from my Chinese food place. I had to have my plain fried rice and plane noodles before I left. They set me up nicely with a job as a director at a Boys and Girls Club near Atlanta. I have always had a love and passion for working with underprivileged kids. I had a hand in raising a lot of my nieces and nephews. So, this was right up my alley.

The next couple of years took a lot of adjustment to go from the street rules and ways of living in St. Louis to the southern hospitality of living in Georgia and a private college. Everyone was so different than the people I was accustomed to being around in St. Louis. Every day I worked out at the Boys and Girls Club in Canton, Georgia, and then I drove over an hour to go to a gym called The Run and Shoot to play basketball. The competition was fierce. It was the right mix of NBA players, high profile college players, and a lot of very experienced overseas professional players. I quickly made friends and got into the hoop circuit.

Being a people person has always been a strength of mine. I met my other big brother from another mother, Kelvin Hamner.

11

Doctor Hamner, that is. Kelvin just finished medical school and was looking to work with athletes. He taught me about nutrition, muscle growth, proper working out techniques, diet, and a lot of things that made me a better athlete and a more knowledgeable person. I also realized that there are a lot of very successful people who don't make millions of dollars. It was amazing to see such a prosperous, black, educated, middle, and upper class of people who were not athletes, rappers, or drug dealers. I was in circles of very influential lawyers, doctors, and businessmen of color. I had never experienced such. I listened and learned a lot from all my new knowledgeable, educated acquaintances, and success associates.

It was then at 21 years old; I start to understand what success looked like and what it consisted of. Everyone I was around was doing what they wanted to do and more so what they set out to do with their lives. Imagine everyone working in jobs and careers that they loved and truly planned to do until they were ready to retire. One thing that everyone agreed on was that when you choose the right career or job, then it will not feel like work at all.

I learned what TRUE SUCCESS was all about very early in life. My Dad truly exemplified the meaning of true success through his attitude, actions, and lifestyle. He was doing exactly what he planned to do with his life. He shared majority of his time with loved ones daily. He was admired and looked up to not only from his family, but by everyone who he met. He was a mentor to many and the go-to-man in the community when there was a problem. For my dad, he knew what true success was for him. To have a loving family who he could provide for, teach, mentor and take care of.

The foundation on which any and all types of success exist begins in your mind. Mental Success requires you to utilize your most significant, powerful asset- your Brain. Your thoughts are your brain's manifestation for desired results. Your desired results are simply goals that you work to achieve. Therefore, it is very important to think positive thoughts as frequent as possible. No matter if it's regarding your ambitions or your failures. I credit my dramatic, impoverished child-hood with making me knowledgeable and well-practiced in decision making. Goal setting is your personal developmental planning of your life ambitions and desires. Goal setting requires practice, the more you do it, the better you become at it. The goals you think about the most are going to greatly increase your odds to successfully accom-plish them.

Just as it holds true for everything that you want to be good at, the more you can practice making good decisions, then the better you will become at it. This holds true with schoolwork, sports, video games, your job, and anything that you desire to be affluent at. No matter how old you are or what your current living situation is, your quality of life is determined by your mental success and your ability set goals with the determination to accomplish them. These two signifi-cant factors greatly impact lively hood. The sooner you recognize that they are very essential determinates of your life's quality, the quicker you can make change in the areas that you want to improve in. TRUE SUCCESS incorporates three major types of success. Mental Success, Physical Success and Financial Success are all equally important. The goal is by the end of this guide, you will not only understand the ben-eficial purpose of achieving the 3 types of success, you will have the knowledge and understanding to create your own personal Blueprint to achieve True Success. If your objective is to unlock the best version of you, then this book is the guide for you.

True Success

MENTAL Success

PHYSICAL Success

FINANCIAL Success

There is only one U in success for a reason

PART 1
MENTAL SUCCESS

Cultivate a mindset for success

in all aspects of your life

Self-Awareness

U become great once U real-ize that U are great.

You are what you think you are. Your self-awareness is a very significant factor in your life's quality. A healthy self-awareness allows you to understand and be accountable for your emotions, thoughts, and behaviors. It is also instrumental when working on your life's objectives and desires. Your goal is to not only have total confidence in your decisions and abilities, but also be able to positively lead by example for others. If you are confident in yourself, you will be able to live a balanced happy life.

I learned how important self-confidence was very early in life. From ages 7 to 11, I was legally homeless. I mostly slept in a car alone with no adult supervision. Majority of the time at night when I went to sleep, I peed on my-self. There was too much activity in my neighborhood that could harm me, so I was scared to get out of the car when it got dark outside. Sometimes when it was very cold, I would urinate on myself to get warm. Because I did not have a means to wash my clothes, I mostly smelled like pee. I never allowed my conditions to make me feel insecure. My self-esteem was very high because I was always very confident in my abilities and my work ethic. In my head, my peers may smell better and wear better clothes, but I was not going to allow anyone to out work me. No matter what the assignment was, I was determined to find the correct answer. If there was an opportunity to help a classmate out, I would jump to it. I concluded that if I made good grades and could help others when needed, the

16

teacher or other students would not bother me about my odor. Never once did I allow my peers who picked on me to discourage me from assisting them when needed. I had mentally conditioned my mind to think that my way of surviving was simple a secret mission that I was chosen to complete because of how smart I was. My high self-esteem never allowed me to worry about others' opinions. If someone told me I stink, my response would be, "I smell normal you just smell to good." Once U are confident in your abilities, and U understand the importance of who U are inside, no one can break or shake your self-esteem.

As I reflect on many occurrences throughout my life, I realized that my strong self-awareness deserves lots of credit for me becoming the person I am today. It has also saved my life on many occasions. There were many split-second decisions that were the difference between life and death for me. A healthy Self-awareness allows U to not only mange your emotions, but thoughtfully be considerate when dealing with other emotions.

As a youth growing up in the hood, the peer pressure to drink and do drugs was highly prevalent. In high school, as a student and as an athlete, the same pressures exist. As a collegiate athlete, it didn't change. As true as an adult the peer pressure to indulge in drugs and alcohol is still very prevalent. I never adhered to any of the pressures not even once. To date, I have never tasted alcohol or used any kind of drugs. Instead of falling suit to what everyone else was doing I choose to lead by example by never doing it. When you are sure of yourself, you have the courage to follow your own path and to led people. Don't allow anyone to discourage U from pursuing your goals and dreams.

College was a brand-new environment for me. This new life with my new friends was refreshing and fun, except for their partying. As amazing as it was to be around people who had similar goals, I could not fully connect because there were a lot of negative traits that I did not agree with or participate in. Every outing included drinking, and, in some cases, smoking weed or other types of drugs. The drug and alcohol use reminded me of the unfortunate aspect of my community, back in St. Louis. I would never partake, and because of this, I could not fully associate myself with them. Still, to this day, I have never had alcohol or used drugs. It is extremely important who and how you spend your time. Are you and your friends playing video games all the time or out drinking? Either choice is not a productive way to support a positive self-perception. You must surround yourself with like-minded people, if you want to be successful. Your friends and the mate you choose to share your life with is very critical to your self-image, and happiness. The same is true with your family. You must love some family members from a distance. Just because you come from the same blood line does not mean that you must follow in their footsteps or spend a lot of time with them, if their value system is different than yours.

Eric Thomas said it best "think about what you think about". I suggest police your mind the same way you do your cell phone. You have the power not to allow someone's death to redirect your life negatively. Being mentally successful is a cerebral choice. This requires one to train your consciousness to always seek a positive outlook on any giving situation. This mindset unlocks the doors to one understanding of the power of the mind and starts you on the golden road to your success. Ultimately you will truly understand you can achieve any goal that you want.

Convert Your Negative Thoughts

For every hour you are anger, you give up sixty minutes of happiness.

Often, I reflected on multiple traumatic experiences, and I would always get emotionally sadden and mentally drained, thinking about them. I realized that these occurrences were just the first of many negative experiences that would help prepare me to understand True Success. Failure and disappointment show the path to success and happiness.

Maintaining a positive outlook has mental and physical effects. People who think and expect the best often are high achievers, because they are better able to push past resistance and achieve their desired goals. There are a few ways to keep your mindset positive.

1. **Start your day with positive affirmations and focus on the good things in your life.** The old saying, "U are what U think" is true.

2. **Find humor in life.** It's not always as bad as it seems. Learn to wear life loosely and laugh at yourself. It'll make life much more enjoyable.

3. **Always remember, you never lose, you learn.** Look at failures as lessons. Think about what you can take away from any given situation and use it to improve.

4. **Transform your negative self-talk into positive self-talk.** When you're being self-critical, stop and turn it around. Instead of saying thinking you're a horrible basketball player think to yourself that you will be better next time.

5. **You are the average of the 4 people you spend the most time with.** Surround yourself with a winning team of friends and family. Your team's attitude and actions should reflect where you want to go. Life is easier with a support system.

Be your biggest fan, as well as your most significant critic. Are you an optimistic or pessimistic thinker? It's all about the mindset. Take a minute to reflect on the amount time that you spend worrying about things that you cannot control. Most people spend a lot of time thinking about problems, while only spending little to no time figuring out how to solve them. Think of solutions rather than problems. One of my best friends, Andy, taught me that every problem has a solution. He was the most positive person I ever knew, because he was in my inner circle I picked up that quality.

From over two decades of working in education I have acquired a ton of experience with converting negative thoughts to positive ones and solving problems. The first thing you may think is that I'm only talking about students, but the reality is that the students were not my biggest clientele. For every student there is a minimum of 2 adults. The two adults typically range from bio logical mom and dad, mom and boyfriend, dad and girlfriend, mom and grandpa, dad and grandmom, grandpa and grandmom you get the picture.

As an educator it is imperative to understand that your job responsibilities range far pass just the students. We are mentors, role models, and positive influences of students and adults. My students, co-workers or parents have never seen me have a bad day. Your thoughts control your actions. Negative thoughts are the kryptonite to anything positive. Make it a habit to always have a positive attitude. Adjust your mindset to create alternative solutions for adverse problems. Your thoughts and perspectives are a reality. Once you understand how powerful, manipulative, and impactful, your thoughts are, then you would never allow negative thoughts to enter your mind. Unfortunately, many people focus on their failures and shortcomings in life, which limits their growth. Focusing on the negatives is very draining, stressful, and counterproductive. The key is to understand that every failure is a segue to an accomplishment. Without failure, there is no way to gauge and appreciate your success. Every situation, rather it dramatic, hurtful or stressful you can choose to reflect on it in a positive lite. Positive thinking not only helps stress management, but ultimately affects your overall life quality. Processing bad things that happen to us and thinking of a positive take away helps in managing life's uncertainties. Things will happen that are out of our control, but how you respond will determine your success rate.

My mom died when I was thirty-five, and it sadden me deeply for a while. How I managed to bring myself back was to not reflect on her passing, instead reflect on the good thing that she brought to my life. If she had not went through her struggles and made me super independent, I would not have become the person that I am today. Everyone has the choice to determine how life's circumstances will impact them. My mom was not involved much with me when I was a child, but she did her best to make it up to me as an adult.

There are two rational options for any and every occurrence in life. Either they chose positive or negative. If you program yourself always to choose a positive outlook, then this will allow you not to be distracted by negative situations or people.

Everyone is not going to share your vision of you, so do not allow them to tarnish or sway your beliefs, concepts, or thoughts about things you hold passionate. Keep your perception of yourself in high regard all the time in all situations. Having self-respect and high esteem will allow you to make sound decisions, accomplish goals, and focus on empowering yourself.

Emotional Intelligence

"Knowledge comes from learning.
Wisdom comes from living."
Anthony Douglas Williams

As we go through life, we all will face challenges. Some of us will fall, and others will sidestep and keep going. The difference between those who allow life circumstances to derail them and those who go on to achieve great success comes down to mastering emotions and using logic to navigate through the obstacle course of life strategically. Do not allow your emotional reasoning to sabotage your logical thought process. Don't get me wrong. Everyone gets upset, but it's how you handle the disappointment that will determine if and how you succeed. The goal is for feelings to be driven in a positive direction instead of a dead-end.

The worst thing in the world that happened to me was my dad and my auntie passing. The first thing I had to do was to not focus on my loved ones passing, but reflect on the positive memories and what I learned from them. In 6 short years of having my dad in my life, I learned the importance of spending time with family, making money, and exercising. From my aunt I learned the significance of teaching, mentoring, and being a loving person to everyone. The first and most important factor in understanding and achieving any type of success is being mentally stable and competent. Your thoughts are the most powerful tool that you control in life. Don't allow situations or people to impact them or persuade them negatively.

Think logically

1. **Train your mind to control your emotions.** Emotional decisions are the reason for majority of your negative circumstances. They also make you lose sight of your objectives. Those driven by emotions are typically unstable, lack confidence, and unpredictable.

2. **Be reasonable in your decision making all the time.** People who are rational in thought and conduct themselves with poise get more respect and become excellent leaders.

3. **Make the type of person you want to be show in your everyday actions.** How you conduct and present yourself should reflect where you want to be in life.

4. **Give respect and consideration to everyone as often as possible.** Aspire to be relatable to many different types of people, but don't compromise who you are.

5. **Don't allow negative people to influence your thought processes.** Never ever lower your standards for someone else approval.

6. **Always think beyond your current circumstances.** Nothing is forever. Where you want to be is only a series of great decisions and a blueprint away.

We are all entitled to our feelings, but the biggest challenge is to OWN your emotions completely and to process them. By doing this, you are allowing yourself to accept what you are feeling without just reacting on them. Next reflect on it. This will allow you to think about another perspective logically. With this type of processing you will be able to easily identify what your feelings are and why you're feeling them.

My first official 9 to 5 job with the Boy Scouts of America taught me that people respond to you and treat you according to how they perceive you. The more confident you are the more people tend to pay attention to you. If your attitude is negative and pessimistic all the time, people tend not to want to socialize or engage with you. If you come off as optimistic and enthusiastic, then people are drawn to you, enjoy being around you, and go out of their way to help you.

Being a professional athlete came with a privileged lifestyle. I was devastated by my injuries that ended my professional basketball career. But I had to hide any negative emotions and feelings about my life in order to be productive at work. I always made it a point to offer to help other co-workers who needed assistance. I never acted like I was above are better than anyone. I stayed humble and volunteered to assist others every chance I got. Emotionally it was challenging to change lifestyles, but I kept logic at the forefront of all my actions and decision making.

.

Create Explanations Instead Of Excuses

Your mistakes do not define you

Developing a goal-oriented mindset helped me stick with tasks I did not like to do, such as reading, science, math, and just sitting in class. Always have great expectations of yourself. Excuses are used to justify not doing better. Everyone should always be learning and growing. By effectively communicating your beliefs and actions, you are not only helping yourself grow, but others as well. Don't accept excuses from others either. Hold people accountable for their own actions.

My later life experiences taught me that your mind is your most essential asset. The mind's significance is it can serve as a tool, weapon, or instrument for any circumstances in life. Imagine your mind as a blank computer with unlimited data storage space. Envision being given access to the Mint where the money is printed. Now, imagine you can go in as much as you like and take out whatever you desire. Of course, you are going to make frequent visits and store as much as you can in your vault. Now, imagine knowledge is the money, and your brain is the vault. Everything you deposit makes you smarter. Don't allow yourself to take days off. Keep continuously filling your trunk. Acquiring knowledge takes unshakable confidence. There is an unlimited supply readily available to everyone.

Most of the people age ten and up have unlimited access to knowledge and data with their cell phones and laptops. Take advantage of your resources by using them to access useful information. Anytime either my students or children ask me a question that they can Google, I point them in that direction. Later I return the same question back to them to make sure that they found the proper answer. Utilizing available resources is critical to becoming a good problem solver. Your willingness to take on new challenges and to expose yourself to new information is a pathway to accomplishing everything that you want.

The saying "Fake it to you make it" is why a lot of people are stuck in complacency. This excuse has stunted growth in many areas for many people. Instead of putting all that time energy and effort into faking like you have it are know it, put in the work to actually learn it or complete it and use the saying "make it so you don't have to fake it."

It is essential to train yourself to be a problem solver. The goal is to develop a problem-solving mindset in all areas of life. The best way to develop this is to practice it frequently. You more than likely already do this with your circle of friends. Certain friends typically come to you with all types of problems and drama with which they need assistance. You usually give your opinion or answers to support them. What you have been doing and not realizing is utilizing your problem-solving skills. You have been practicing this a good majority of your life.

Now you must turn your attention to yourself and deal with your issues. Every problem has an answer. The key is to put in the time and effort to solve it. Learn from the friends that you go to for advice about your issues. Make it a point to hang out with them as much as you can. Even if you can't physically hang out, stay in contact with them. These friends are typically on the ball and focused. Learn from their good habits.

Now for your friends who are emotionally, financially, and or physically depressed, the goal is to assist them without allowing it to drain you. Don't allow them to be your excuse for not working to your potential. Try to support them and figure out why their problem exists and how they can resolve it? At the same time, learn from their mistakes.

As I reflected on the people around me when I entered the 9 to 5 work force, I must give credit to them for showing me all the things that I should not do. Majority of the people were miserable with their lives and their jobs, so their demeanor was negative. I also must credit myself with not following in their footsteps. I learned a lot from their mistakes. I have observed and listened to so many people give excuses for what they were not doing are why they were not where they felt they should be that I compiled resolutions for them in case I had the same issues. The key is turn mistakes and failures to lessons.

In school, it's easy to go with the flow and follow suit with your classmates and friends who only want to be average. When you decide to be better, smarter, and more focused you, will see a positive change in all areas that U want to improve. Make it a point to hang with students who are making the good grades and have similar goals. Challenge yourself to increase class participation, focus, and behavior. Communicate with your teachers when you need assistance. Strengthen your habits and time management. Adopt these skills and you will achieve better in all areas of life.

On the job, there are always a million things that could be better. The question is, are you able to give a million solutions? The chances are that you are not. As a rule of thumb, make it a point to only associate yourself with issues that you can resolve or come up with explanations to. Being a problem solver will make you a lot more resourceful and promotable. This factor is the difference between your current position and the one you desire. People who create explanations run and own companies. The people who create excuses work for people who own companies. It is totally up to you.

Everyone makes mistakes or do things that others don't agree with, but instead of making excuses, explain your thought process behind what you do and why you do it. By using effective communication and explaining yourself, you open the door to other options.

Sometimes it's best to sit and listen or own the fact you made a mistake and keep it moving. When you feel like there's more to the story, explain yourself instead of using excuses. Taking the time to explain the reasoning behind your actions will open more options for explanations than excuses. Offering an explanation opens the line of positive communication, which helps people understand you or the situation better. By having a better understanding, they're able to help you fix the problem or to not repeat the mistake. It also opens others' eyes to another perspective that may not have been considered.

When all else fails, apologize and move on when you feel it's needed. A heartfelt apology can go a very long way in repairing, sustaining, and building relationships with others. Lastly, believing in yourself means understanding yourself and having the ability to communicate your actions. Great communicators who own their actions and can explain themselves thoroughly have a higher percentage achieving goals.

How to Create a Strong Mindset

Fall seven times, stand up eight

Think of your brain as a factory, and your thoughts are the merchandise that your mind is manufacturing. You are the owner of the factory, so the success of your factory is dependent upon what you allow your factory to produce. If you are not in control of your thoughts, then human nature takes control, and before you're even aware of what's happening, you are stressing about things that you can't control, and taking on stress that does not involve you. Tough situations can consume your mind, and instead of figuring out how to get out, the negative situation traps you. How you perceive any given life situation or circumstance will determine how you handle it.

There is a saying that the only thing that is certain in life is death and taxes, I like to add adversity to the saying. Adversity will certainly show up in your life at some point. Having a strong mindset prepares you to take on any and all obstacles. A tried and true statement is "Get your mind right". Unfortunately, today a lot of people do not take the time to do so. The way to accomplish getting your mind right is to formulate your blueprint for things that you want to accomplish in life as early as possible. Your definition of success does not need to be measured by anyone other than you.

A strong mindset is emphasizing what you can do and mastering that instead of allowing what you can't do to deter you. In addition, being positive, instead of dwelling on the negative, and learning to move past mental and physical disappointments. As sure as the sun heat is hot you will have many disappointments in life. The key to creating a positive strong mindset is how you react to any given situation.

I was in my twenties when the doctor told me that I could not play basketball anymore. I was devastated. Not only had basketball allotted me a plush lifestyle but it was my career choice, that I had planned to do for forever. In addition to that my son was just born and I had to figure out what was my next move since basketball was no longer an option for making money. Even worst I did not have a backup plan. This really added to my devastation. I was in the sunken place for a couple of months and saw my savings running full speed toward 0. I sat down and wrote a list of jobs that I wanted to have. Next, I calculated an amount that would allow me to comfortably support my family. Then, I made a list of jobs that I were interested in and researched their starting salaries. I recall feeling extremely discouraged. All the jobs that I wanted to apply for involved helping people or mentoring kids, but none of them paid enough money to support my family. I refused to allow that to detour me. So, I created an additional list of part time jobs that I could work along with my full-time job. I worked two jobs for years to make sure that my family was taken care of and save some money. I later realized that this was the first Blueprint that I had created and executed.

A healthy mindset is accepting the fact that things will not happen overnight, but the accumulation of small successes over time will help you to achieve big successes. A strong mindset focuses on what you can do instead of what you can't. It's the thought process that cheers you on and keeps you going even in the face of adversity. It's thinking in the present instead of trying to change the past. It doesn't overwhelm you into thinking that everything must be perfect. Instead, it sets you up for success because success is a process that takes time and consistent effort.

A healthy mindset removes roadblocks that prevent forward motion. It keeps you focused on task and in the present with a focus on the future. This mindset will draw strength and wisdom from the past mistakes and failures. A healthy mindset maps out a plan for achievement. It tells you to pick yourself back up when you fall. It does not stay in a dark place too long but envisions a bright future. A healthy mind is strategic. It guides you through steps necessary to navigate pitfalls and guides you up mountains until you reach the peak of success. A healthy mind is resilient despite physical fatigue. It keeps hoping, planning and driving you to keep going. It tells you the impossible is possible for you if you keep trying. It also builds your confidence, self-esteem, and sharpens your critical thinking skills.

Mental Success BLUEPRINT

"The meaning of life Is to find your gift.
The purpose of life Is to give It away."
Pablo Picasso

Quality decision making is the key to a mental success. Everything is an extension of your actions, so having an actionable game plan will set you up for the goals you desire. If you can visualize objective, you can achieve it. Decide the type of person you want to see yourself as in the future? Start with a vision and then write it down. Break your goal down into doable steps. Come up with a realistic time frame for the completion of each step. Consistently achieving small goals will eventually lead you to your ultimate large ones.

Here are the traits that should make up your Mental Success Blueprint.

1. **Self-confidence, self-esteem, and self-respect are significant factors in your mental success.** How you feel about yourself will determine how you react to people and how you react to situations. The key is to harness your inner drive and continue to reinforce it with a definite purpose and focus on achieving your goals.

2. **Think before you speak.** Your spoken words are very powerful, so talk to others as you would like to be talked too.

3. **No matter what your circumstances are, always be mindful that you have the power to change them.** Believe in yourself and your abilities.

4. **Utilize the resources available.** Learn to be resourceful. Always attempt to solve problems on your own.

5. **Ask for help only when you have attempted to solve the issue at minimum 3 times on your own.** Don't be afraid of failure remember it is a seque to your next successes.

6. **Don't judge yourself simply by where you're from.** How you are perceived is not from where you come from, but how you act and treat others.

7. **Be willing to help people without expecting anything in return.** Make sure that you help people whenever you can. Good people attract good people.

8. **Don't judge a book by its cover.** You should never look down on other people because of where they are from or how they look.

9. **Be humble.** Material wealth does not make you better than anyone. What defines a person is what they do with what they have, and how they help others along the way.

10. Your Brain is your most important asset. Your mind has great potential and the more you use it the better it becomes. So, if you are constantly learning you are perpetually growing.

11. Problem solving is one of the most important skills you can learn. The most successful people are those who can solve problems.

12. Things will not always go as planned. There will be a lot of times were things are going bad. Stay calm during the storm. Some of the most successful people endured the greatest struggles.

13. Change the narrative with your suffering. You have the power to allow it to bring out the best in you. Use negative situations as extra motivation to reach goals.

14. Set yourself up for achievement. To bring your vision of the life U want to fruition, you must go after success with unwavering focus. Surround yourself with people who are as determined to pursue their goals as hard as you do.

15. Never compromise yourself or your beliefs to fit in. Your value system is what makes you special even if it sets you apart from others.

16. Spend your time wisely. Everyone lives in the same 24-hour time block. The most affluent successful people spend their time on things that will move them forward. It's so easy to get caught up in activities that are time wasters like social media, video games, and watching TV. For every minute U spend on mindless activities triple that time reading a book or working on achieving a goal.

17. **Monitor your thoughts.** Think about what you're thinking about. Be aware when your mind wanders and cycles through a negative thought pattern. Condition yourself to pause, reflect and redirect your mind to positive thinking.

18. **What others think of you is none of your business.** Don't allow people negative thoughts to influence your actions.

19. **Don't compare your life to others.**

20. **Make all the above actions a habit.** As holds true for anything that you want to be great at, practice makes perfect and positive thinking is a healthy habit worth working towards.

PART 2
PHYSICAL SUCCESS

The body U want is built one

good decision after another

Healthy Habits

U are your body's architect

Growing up in sports taught me a few healthy habits that have really allowed me to keep myself fit. One that dates to my teenage years is doing push-ups or squats anytime I was in class tired or bored at work. I also did them during TV commercials. Coach Hunt, my AAU basketball trainer, told me to do this to build muscle, since I did not have consistent access to any type of gym. This habit, I have passed along to my students, fitness clients, and kids over the years. For those who cannot do neither, you can adjust it to do almost any type of movement or exercise that you like. Another one that has helped me through many classes, meetings, and lectures is going to the bathroom or some private place to do jumping jacks or any exercise that gets the blood flowing and wakes you up. This is also an awesome method that I use to help my students stay active and alert in class.

Best practice when building healthy habits require simple motion routines. For instance, I purposely make sure to not use assistance when I get up or sit down. I also do it multiple times every hour that by the end of the day I have completed at least 60 reps. Small activities of this sort make a big difference in staying fit. Even now as an adult, I do not ride elevators, I elect to take the stairs as much as possible. Small decisions add up over time to create a healthy mind set. Healthy habit formation is the foundation of wellness. You must determine what you want your identity to be and then frame your lifestyle around it. Everywhere I go people look at me and assume I play a professional sport, or I do something with fitness. This is a confidence boost as well as external motivation to stay healthy for me. Figure out what is a motivator for you. For some people it's sports, others it's vanity or ego. No matter what it takes to motivate you, make healthy habits a priority.

Forming Healthy Habits takes consistency and goal setting just like anything else that you want to accomplish. Your habits will be anchors in place to support the goals you want to achieve. Create an environment that supports your habits. For example, I have an entire gym in my bedroom. So as soon as I wake up I do a little workout, and before I go to bed I do another, daily. Making fitness routine, allows you to not have to rely purely on determination and will-power. If it's a routine, then every environment will support it.

Take a good look around you. What parts of your life need changing to support your long-term fitness goals? Break those goals down into small actionable steps. For example, you may decide that you want to do 200 squats a week at school or at work. Or you may want to do 25 sitting stomach crunches every hour for 8 hours a day? By practicing these steps frequently, you will be creating healthy lifestyle habits.

It's best practice to personalize the habits you'd like to focus on. Here are a few basics that everyone should consider.

1. **Adequate Sleep** - Everyone should strive for 7-9 hours of sleep at night. The best way to accomplish this is to set a bedtime routine and adhere to it.

2. **Manage Stress** - Incorporate a little time for reflection into your daily life. It can be as little as 5 minutes a few times a day. Don't allow yourself to get worked up about small things.

3. **Drink Adequate Water** - Strive for 1/2 your body weight in ounces of water and drink when you are

thirsty. To help you measure your consumption you should have some sort of water bottle or container.

4. **Eat the Rainbow** - Add a variety of colors to your nutrition. You can do this by eating adequate fruits and vegetables. Strive for 5-7 servings a day.

5. **Use Portion Control** - Portioning your food can save you calories and your waistline. A good strategy is to use a smaller plate and fill at least half the plate with vegetables. I personally eat out of my kids small 3 portion plates.

6. **Eat Adequate Protein** - Protein is the building block of the body. It will also help you feel full longer. I personally eat about 4 hard boiled egg whites a day. I also eat them late at night if I'm hungry and don't want to eat a big meal.

7. **Daily Exercise** - Get at least 30 minutes of exercise a day. Make this a priority, like brushing your teeth and showering.

8. **Stretch Daily** - Stretching will help you move better and prevent injuries. If you have never tried yoga, give it a chance. Yoga has made a significant difference for me, my kids, my students, and my clients.

9. **Rest between Workouts** - Rest is just as important as exercise. It helps your body repair itself and builds endurance for the next workout.

10. Plan and Prepare your Meals at Home - Meal planning and prepping your food at home is a healthier option than eating out, and it saves money.

These are some basic healthy habits that would benefit anyone. Come up with some of your own to fit into your health goals. Remember consistency is your best friend in health. The goal is to live a long healthy life.

How To Eat

Eat the Rainbow

There are a lot of different theories on what and how you should eat to be healthy. In my research, I have found portion control to be a very important factor in eating healthy. I love to use kid plates with the parts sectioned off to control my portions. When I'm out, I use the palm of my hand method. Basically, each potion of food should be around the same size as the palm of my hand. Not only should you focus on how much you eat, but also on what you eat. I enjoy a variety of foods, but I am very conscientious about how much and how often I eat foods that are not healthy and desserts. I love eating and I love food with flavor, so I make it a point to only indulge in food that I like. For instance, I love seafood such as crab legs, lobster, and scallops. Unfortunately, all of these are high in sodium and cholesterol, so I make sure not to indulge too often. I also make sure that my follow-up meal is extremely healthy, like salad. Sometimes I use food to reward myself. For instance, I love Dairy Queen ice cream cake. When I say love, I mean to the point where anytime my kids or anyone in my family has a birthday I bring ice cream cake. Anytime that I am going to have ice cream cake, about two days before, I double up my cardio workout. With this system in place, anytime I am going to eat something that is not healthy I make myself earn it though more exercise.

Eating well is not as complicated as many try to make it seem. The easiest way to explain is to eat what the earth naturally produces, like fruits, vegetables, seeds, nuts, and beans. "Eating the Rainbow" is a concept that encourages eating a variety of colorful nutrient-dense fruits and vegetables daily, so the body gets the nutrition it needs to stay healthy. Each day aim for at least five servings of fruits and vegetables. Yes, smoothies and supplements with these natural items count. Another critical thing to focus on is staying hydrated. This is equally as important as eating the rainbow. At least 60% of the human body is water, so for it to function correctly, consume adequate water daily. Aim for half your body weight in ounces and drink when thirsty. If you stick to consuming what Mother Nature provides, you'll be sure to stay on a healthy track. Here are a few more helpful dietary suggestions:

1. **Eat lots of vegetables and fruits.** Think about the colors in a rainbow and choose a fruit or vegetable for each color to give yourself options. Salads are a great way to get a lot of daily servings of fruits and veggies.

2. **Stay away from processed foods**. Eating food in its original form gives you the benefits of all the nutrients and allows you to avoid the extra salt, sugar, and fat added to processed food.

3. **Drink adequate water.** One of the most essential factors to good health is water. Your organs and cells need water to function properly. Water gets rid of waste and toxins from your body through urination, perspiration and bowel movements.

4. **Cook at home as frequent as possible.** Plan and prepare healthy meals weekly for lunch if your able. When you must or choose to eat out elect to order the healthy items that are available. For instance, I

love Chick-fil-A, but I make sure to order grilled chicken or salad.

5. **Minimize sweets.** Fresh fruit has an enough natural sugar to neutralize any sweet crave. My go to fruits are Mangos and Grapes.

6. **Don't skip meals because it will lead to overeating.** Use portion control to manage how much you eat and eat smaller meals more frequently. Instead of 3 big meal a day eat four to five smaller meals.

7. **When eating out, choose healthy foods**. My suggestion is to pull the menu online first so you can make sure that healthy options are available.

8. **Be a healthy example for others when eating in groups.** Don't allow peer pressure to affect what you eat. Teach everyone around you about healthy eating habits.

9. **Learn how to cook.** Learning to cook is as important as learning to drive, that is if you want to be able to control your health destination.

10. **Stick to lean protein.** Egg whites are a great source of protein, and a healthy snack.

11. **Be mindful of the calories in things you drink.** Often a good majority of unwanted calories come from the beverages that you consume. Check out the calories in the drinks that you frequent.

How To Work Out

Exercise is the architect. Rest is the builder. Nutrition is the foundation.

The number one rule of your exercise agenda is working out should be fun and challenging. Make a point to pick something you can do consistently. A well-rounded exercise program should consist of these components.

Stretching and Flexibility:

Stretching and flexibility is essential for proper mobility. It's also essential for injury prevention. For all sports it improves performance. Stretching should be done daily, in the morning, before and after exercise, and at night. This is one thing that you should make a habit of. No matter If you are an athlete or someone who never works out, stretching and flexibility are very important.

Cardiorespiratory Training:

Cardiorespiratory training keeps the heart strong and healthy. It also improves lung function and increases the sense of well-being. Proper cardio training also helps prevent illnesses such as cancer, diabetes, heart disease, stroke, and many others. In all aspects of life cardio training is beneficial. I like to do mine first thing in the morning, Even before I brush my teeth, I go and get on the elliptical. This in turn energizes me for the entire day.

Core and Balance:

Training your core is the foundation. The nucleus is power center and balance system of your body. Keeping the core strong will help you move more efficiently, perform better, and prevent injury. All movements power source is from your core.

Resistance Training:

Resistance training uses bands, free weights, weighted balls, or your body weight. Its purpose is to make you stronger, but there are many more benefits, including improved joint function, increased bone density, enhanced immune function, and a stronger cardiovascular system. Working out should start slowly and build endurance and strength progressively.

Below are few other tips for working out:

1. Resting is a critical component for injury prevention and strength progression.

2. Allow at least 48 hours between strength training a body part, except the core. You can train the core every day.

3. Concentrate on consistency. Having a regular workout schedule allows you to incorporate working out into your daily lifestyle.

4. If you are hurt, do not push past pain, but spend time recovering. Get assessed by a doctor and go to therapy if necessary.

5. Remember, there are no quick fixes or short cuts to physical fitness. Slow progress wins over going hard and getting injured.

6. Design a plan that's doable with built in progression. If you need help, hire a trainer for accountability, knowledge, and for the added push.

7. Sports are a good way to stay active and have fun. Join a league of a sport that you enjoy. I play in a few basketball and volleyball leagues year-round. It is a great way to keep me motivated to stay in shape.

8. Choose leisure time that also incorporates physical activity like biking, golf, swimming, etc.

Dance Freely
And Frequently

Dance like no one is watching.

Dancing is one of the biggest fitness secrets. In my opinion, it is the coolest way to burn calories and get family fun time for all ages. There is something about grooving to a favorite song that seems to take care away. Not only is dancing great for shedding calories but it also has social benefits. Research shows that it can also improve mental, emotional, and physical well-being.

How many times have you been at a party or some type of gathering and wishing you could dance like the cool confident people on the dance floor? Socially, dancing is inclusive. If you can move, you can dance. So, if you shy away from other forms of exercise, try dancing. It's a great way to have fun, meet people, and get moving. I have always enjoyed dancing. In most cases I'm the only 6'6 260lb guy on the dance floor moving and grooving off beat, but I love it and I'm sure by the end of the night I have burned 100s of calories.

Mentally, dancing is a mood booster because it increases feel-good hormones. It's a great way to escape the demands of life and let loose even if it's just for a short while. I have always made it a point to volunteer to chaperone all the school's dances, so I could show my moves. The only way friends and family can get me out the house to go out is if there is a dance floor.

Emotionally, dancing is very expressive and helps release pent up emotions through movement. Dancing also helps decrease symptoms of anxiety, depression, stress, and boosts self-esteem. It safe to say that me and my kids and I spend about 20 minutes a day dancing, even if it's while we prepare a meal are clean up. Dancing puts a little fun and movement to almost any task. We also do talent shows that allows them to be creative with dance.

Physically, dancing improves the cardiovascular system, strengthens bones, and enhances balance and strength. It also can improve brain function by memorizing favorite dance moves and patterns. When I go out dancing, I go in the club dry and come out soaked in sweat. Regardless of your age, anyone can benefit from dance, so get moving and grooving on the regular. Below are a few more suggestions about dancing.

1. Dancing is not only fun, but a great workout and is good for the heart. Think of dancing as your own personal workout that you create and control the paste of your movements.

2. Dancing helps with balance and coordination. During my professional years of basketball, we had to take Latin dance during the off season.

3. It helps with burning calories and supports muscle memory. The newer moves you learn the more muscle groups you work out.

4. Zumba is an awesome way for anyone to get started dancing. The first time I did Zumba I thought that I was going to have to be carried to my car.

5. Incorporate dance and music when you clean the house, your room, the bathroom or any area. Any added energy expenditure can burn calories.

6. Take a dance class. After being exposed to Latin dance, I learned African, Ballroom, and Hip-Hop dance.

7. Dancing is good for your mental health. It is a safe way for you to express your emotions and to release negative energy. It can also mentally prepare you for certain types of competitions are challenges.

8. Fact that most people do not know is dancing doesn't take any special talent, just move and have fun.

9. Dancing is enjoyment and exercise for all ages and all stages of life.

Leisure Time

Rest and recharge your body for optimal function.

Living in survival mode for many years made me very resilient and determined to be successful. Mentally my mind would never turn off and physically I would push myself to know end. This was not healthy because I would not allow myself to have any free time. I was an official workaholic. I realized when things got better that one cannot and should not exist like this long-term. It's not healthy for the body to be under constant stress. No matter what age you are, stress is your enemy. Lack of sleep puts a lot of undue stress on your body. Long hours on the job or on video games all put a large amount of stress on your mind and body. Rest and relaxation are just as much about health as exercise and nutrition. Make it a priority to find healthy outs for your free time.

Adequate sleep and stress management are both often overlooked when making wellness changes. As an adult, I can appreciate the downtime afforded to me after working so hard all my life. It makes me healthier, happier, and more productive. My favorite down time is hanging out with my kids. It does not matter if I am coaching a sport that they play are just watching a movie. I also am an advocate of restorative naps. Typically, when I must coach two separate sports teams of my kids on the same day, a nap is in my schedule.

I also like swimming because studies have shown that it helps dissipate negative energy. Over the years, I've incorporated low impact exercises that are great for the joints, muscles and psyche, like yoga and Pilates. In addition to some low-key leisure activities, I also stay healthy doing fun, recreational activities like basketball league and bowling. Biking is also great because it's a great cardiovascular workout without the impact. Leisure time can be any activity you enjoy that makes you feel relaxed and balanced. I personally love to play Monopoly and almost any card game with my kids, friends, and family.

Many years of working hard and making good decisions have allowed me to reap the benefits of lots of family time. I also make time for friends and occasional solo trips to help me rest and recharge. The recharge allows me to be able to continue to tackle all that life has to offer with a balanced mindset and positive outlook. Remember to slow down and appreciate life. You only get one.

Leisure time applies to everyone, no matter what age you are, what position you work, or what stage of life you are going in. Here is a recap of things that you should be mindful of.

1. Leisure time is essential for your mind and body.

2. It is proven to help reduce stress and manage depression.

3. Relaxation allows you to refuel and regroup.

4. Some leisure activities can be sportive and good for your physical well-being, such as bicycling, bowling, golfing, hiking/walking, skating, skiing, and swimming.

5. If you prefer a slower pace leisure time that nurtures the mind, consider painting, drawing, reading, or one of my favorites listen to music.

6. Traveling is also an excellent way to experience leisure time. It's a vacation from everyday life that allows you to recharge and come back refueled.

7. If you like the outdoors, consider camping, or going to the beach.

Leisure time ultimately improves the quality of your life, so be sure to take the time to pamper and treat yourself. You deserve it for working so hard.

PHYSICAL SUCCESS BLUEPRINT

Quality decision making is the key to a physical success. Everything is an extension of your actions, so having an actionable game plan will set you up for the goals you desire. If you can visualize objective, you can achieve it. Decide how you want to see yourself in the future? Start with a vision and then write it down. Break your goal down into doable steps. Come up with a realistic time frame for the completion of each step. Consistently achieving small goals will eventually lead you to your ultimate large ones.

Achieving optimum wellness takes establishing habits like eating well, exercising, getting adequate sleep, and managing stress. Placing the focus on these foundational health habits will enable you to achieve your highest physical potential. For you to function at your best, you must take care of yourself. If you don't, at some point, you'll plateau or worse. Eventually, you may crash or develop an avoidable illness such as obesity, heart diseases, high blood pressure, or diabetes.

Below are helpful suggestions to help you create your blueprint.

1. Physical success should encompass mind and the body.

2. It's about managing your overall health to achieve longevity and quality of life.

3. Mindset hugely affects how the body functions, so finding balance and making peace a priority will increase your physical success.

4. Nurturing the mind with positive thoughts and limiting negative external exposures to the body like drugs and alcohol.

5. Stay physically active everyday by doing things you enjoy.

6. Go outside and get fresh air and sunshine. Vitamin D does the body good.

7. Make sure you rest adequately because in order for the body to function properly it needs down time to repair.

8. Exercise is the architect, rest is the builder and nutrition is the foundation.

9. (Strive for 5) servings of vegetables daily.

10. Limit your consumption of processed foods.

11. Use portion control to manage your food intake and eat until satisfied and not stuffed.

12. Drink adequate water with a goal of half your body-weight in ounces of water and when thirsty.

13. Eat for life and learn to cook healthy versions of your favorite foods.

14. Learn to incorporate your surrounds in your workout.

15. Motion and moving is your ally.

16. A high priced gym membership is useless without commitment, drive, consistency, and a plan.

17. If you have physical limitations, work around what you can't do and focus on what you can do. For example, if you have a knee injury, bike instead of run. If you have a shoulder or back injury, swim instead of playing sports.

18. Be safe, modify your activity and keep going.

19. Make the most of your time anyplace is a good place to work out. For instance, on breaks at work walk the steps.

20. Create different places to work-out, so you're never bored.

21. Keep exercise equipment at home, get your steps in at work, buy a gym membership, or play on a recreational team to stay motivated.

22. Challenge yourself physically, set goals often.

Overall wellness is achieved through proper nutrition it helps to chart your efforts.

Below are a few samples of some graphic organizers that can assist you in your journey to physical success.

Nutrition Goal - Eat the Rainbow
5 Servings of Fruits and Veggies a Day

Drink Adequate Water (half bodyweight in ounces of water)

Water Tracker (oz)	Veggie Tracker	Fruit Tracker

Exercise at least 30 minutes daily

Type of Exercise	Minutes

EXPLORE YOUR PASSION

List the Activities You like Best

Practice What You Love Daily

PART 3

FINANCIAL SUCCESS

Don't measure your success

using someone else's ruler

Money Mindset

U are the secret to your success

A money mindset is an attitude that you have about your finances. It's the driving force for making decisions about your money.

As a kid, I learned to value money because I earned every penny through blood, sweat, and tears. It was very important that every nickel I made was assigned to a meaningful purchase. I knew what it was like to be broke and that feeling was very stressful and enabling. Necessities, a bite to eat, and a warm, safe place to stay was my primary objective. I learned from my past, and that's what taught me how to access financial freedom. I learned the importance of managing money, buying what I could afford, and purchasing what made sense all by age 13.

I can remember exactly when I lost my way and started making emotional money decisions. I decided to buy any and everything that I ever wanted. I gave myself a financial goal and laid out a blueprint to achieve it. I gave myself 24 months to accomplish it. With basketball money no longer an option and slim to no chance of hitting the lottery, I understood that I had to put some work in. I went back to school to get my master's and certification to secure a teaching job. I quickly moved up the ranks to administrator and every dime I could afford I used to started investing in real estate and stocks. With earnings from those ventures I purchased a car lot. Although I was making good money, I knew that I could make more. I went back to school to get a personal training certification and started fitness training. I noticed that all of my clients got massaged regularly, so I went back to school to learn massage. At this stage, people around me noticed that I was making money and wanted to know how I was doing it, so I started doing financial consulting. I made myself a one stop shop for almost everything. You could come to me to buy a house, car, fix your credit, get trained, massage, and tutored. I surpassed my goal within 18 months. This amount allowed me to achieve every materialistic goal that I ever could imagine. Without thinking logically, I purchased everything that I ever wanted, dreamed of, are fantasized about.

The first thing I wanted to do was buy my mom a new house. I went to her first and attempted to move her out of the old neighborhood, but she would not budge. Although I was wise beyond my years in many ways, I still had a poverty mindset. The poverty mindset is when you buy a bunch of things that you desire that do not add any value to your net worth. You make a lot of big financial emotional decisions instead of smart calculated investments. I decided to buy everything that I ever wanted and ever dreamed of. I built a mansion with an indoor pool and I didn't even know how to swim. I had an eight-car garage and I only owned two cars at the time I built the house. Of course, I ended buying 5 more cars to justify my garage. As if that 10,000 sq foot mansion was not enough I also had 3 other personal homes in places I visited maybe twice a year.

My poverty fostered financial irresponsibility, which back to bite me in the 2008 recession. I learned a hard-expensive lesson by ignoring the money mindset that allotted me the success I had achieved. The good thing was that I learned and earned a greater appreciation for the value of money all over again as an adult entrepreneur. I also realized that I did not have to be a professional athlete to make the type of money that would allow me to live how I wanted.

Figure out what is your financial Why? The most critical factor in financial success is knowing your financial WHY? Your financial why is the amount you need to make consistently to live the life you desire. Once you have decided an amount that will allow you to live the type of life you want for yourself, then you may begin setting up your strategic plan (Blueprint). Having a positive money mindset requires specific attributes such as:

1. **Value your talents and place a price on them.** Don't allow people to pay you less then you are worth. Remember all salaries are negotiable, all contracts are negotiable, and almost anything dealing with money is negotiable.

2. **Create multiple streams of income.** Work as many jobs as you need to in order to reach your financial goals. Even with owning multiple businesses generating 6 figures, anytime I need to achieve a monetary goal I work a fulltime job, I drive Uber, Lift, do fitness training, and massage to hit my financial target.

3. **Learn everything about the business you are in and study your trade continuously.** The knowledge you gain is priceless and transferrable.

4. **Make a financial percentage blueprint.** This will allow you to give your money purpose. Keep a financial planner and track your ins and outs.

5. **Read. Read, Read.** Educate yourself on money management. Learn how to save and invest, so you can make your money work for you. Learn about as many things as you can regarding money, investing, and financial literacy.

6. **Learn what Debt is and how it effects your financial life.** Too often we learn about debt the hard way,

that is when we create a bunch of bad debt and we have no workable plan to get out of it. The more you know and understand about it, the less likely you are to create too much of it.

7. **Utilize credit cards as financial assets**. Credit Cards are a great way to build credit history, but only if you are paying the balance off monthly. They are also useful if you get ones that pay you cash back for purchases are have other types of value incentives.

8. **Get a mentor who can teach you money management.** Your mentor can be a person, a book, or any source that helps you with financial literacy. Today there is a wealth of resources on this topic, if you do not have a person mentor accessible. Even with my success, I have a few mentors that I constantly look to and learn things from.

9. **Post daily affirmations that reflect what you want financially.** Seeing is believing. What you think about drives your thoughts and actions.

10. **Invest money in things that appreciate like real estate.** In my opinion and many other successful entrepreneurs' opinion real estate is golden. People will always need a place to live.

I have only mentioned a few methods I used to obtain a consistent stream of income. Some ways were creative, others done out of desperation, but they all were for a purpose. Make sure to give your money a purpose. My suggestion is using a percentage blueprint for all the money you receive. My percentage Blueprint is broken down like this, 25% of every dollar I own goes to savings, 30% is for me to live off which includes food, shelter, bills and entertainment, 45% is to reinvest. Using this type of Blueprint gives your money purpose.

The knowledge I gained during uncertain times and from my failures has been extremely valuable in my success. I learned how to manage money, how to save money, and how to make a dollar stretch. For instance, while everyone was buying one pair of fancy high-priced shoes, I would buy 5 pairs of no name shoes. The logic was simple, 5 pair would last a lot longer than 1 pair. I learned from other people mistakes, and that taught me financial literacy.

The earlier you start managing your money the better you become at it. If you make smart spending a habit early your money will go a long way. Don't make excuses for emotional purchases like new cars if you have not properly saved and worked it into your budget. My rule of thumb with buying cars is that I have to be able to pay for it in cash. Make your monthly saving match your highest outgoing bill. For example, if your mortgage is rent is 1000 then you should be able to save at least 1001 a month. This will assure that you are paying yourself first as well as the most from your earnings. If you start this at a young age, then as you became an adult, you will continue to learn and understand the importance of making money, saving money, and even more importantly, making good decisions with the money you make. The financial decisions you make today will determine how successful your tomorrow looks.

Once you have the money basics down, the next important step is figuring out how to make your money work for you. You will learn more about this in the "Put your Money to Work for You" section.

Parents: Teach your kids to make good money decisions and teach them how to invest. All my kids have stock portfolios that they have a hand in managing. Make it a point to have conversations with your kids about big purchases that they want you to make. Take advantage of all teachable moments with them.

Kids: You can start creating the money mindset by saving portions of your birthday and holiday money. Its never to early to make sound financial decisions. I remember my daughter was six and she made $139 dollars making and selling slime, without my assistance.

Find a job are career U love

The biggest determinate for your job or career choice should be, are you happy with what you're doing? If you were financially able, would you do your job for free. Understand that your life quality is not based on how much money you make, but more so what you do with it.

Take advantage of every opportunity

I went to college on a full basketball scholarship and did work study to make money. I combined it with my Pell grant money and invested into the stock market. It was not a lot of money, but by the end of my 4 years I graduated and had made over 40 thousand dollars earned from my investing.

Be positive, persistent in thought, and action.

Around age 14 I decided that I wanted to learn how to play basketball. Not only did I decide that I wanted to learn how to play the game, but I also decided that I wanted to be a professional player someday. Now with the vision in place, I had to learn the basics. I was familiar with the rules, but I did not know how to dribble, shoot, pass, or play defense without fouling. I figured the most important thing to learn is how to play defense. My logic was if I'm able to stop people from scoring, I will always be useful and get picked up to play on people's teams. Next, I concluded that I need to know how to shoot that way I would not be a offensive liability to my team. Once I had achieved those two goals, I added the dribbling and passing to my game. Next, I decided that I would try out for my freshman basketball team. I worked hard and made it. By the end of the season, I was moved up to JV. I thought I was doing well until the next year I was cut from Varsity. I did not let this kill my dream. I set a goal to not only play the next year, but to make all conference. I worked out even harder, switched schools my senior year, and became an all-conference player. My next goal was to get a college scholarship, I continued to work and improve, and I earned a scholarship to Forest Park Community College. Ironically my dad took classes there, so it really meant a lot to me.

Being a success is not only affected by your actions, but it can also be determined by the people who are around you. My best friend and brother from another Mother, Raymond, went to college at the Forest Park Community College and he encouraged me to do the same. I knew nothing about college except that rich people went there. I was never truly a big fan of going to college, but I understood that it was necessary to reach my overall goals. Raymond taught me everything I needed to know to be prepared for college and helped me secure a basketball scholarship to Forest Park CC.

Take a close look at the people around you. Are they interested in the same things you are? Do they focus on positive things like learning and playing sports or are their conversations about things that don't fit into where you are or want to be? As a young adult I think of my best friend Tony. We were basically twin brothers born from different mothers. Tony was a star college basketball player who mentored, inspired, and assisted me to become a star athlete as well. Support matters. Therefore, finding a mentor is an excellent way to get the guidance you need to conquer your goals. A mentor can act as an advisor and a support system to keep you on track and to have your back as you climb the latter of success. Lastly, when making any decision, ask yourself if it will bring you further away or closer to your goals, and act accordingly. Think great. Be great.

Financial GOAL Setting

Goals are dreams with a deadline.

Growing up without necessities caused me to have a Kobe Bryant Mamba like mindset when it came to money. I was relentless in figuring out different ways to make money. This mindset is what fueled the endless hustling to keep acquiring not only the things I needed but also the items I wanted. Unfortunately, without actual financial planning and a goal, the focus was only on materialistic acquisition of depreciable goods such as cars, clothes, personal homes, and high-priced jewelry. I placed value on what I looked like, how many homes I had, and what cars I drove. My priority was only to impress. I felt that since I could not play basketball anymore, I had to still live up to the life associated with it.

There are a lot of people with this attitude. Especially with social media in society today. Unfortunately, for many the trending thought process is to look like you have money although you don't. Many do not want to work hard to achieve it naturally. Spending money and using credit beyond one's means to boost self-esteem has long term negative consequences. This factor alone has diminished many people's finances and their credit.

When I was young, I set personal monetary goals for my mowing service. I figured out how much money I needed to get food and gas for the week. I set an attainable goal of cutting a few yards on every street in my neighborhood. Successfully reaching my goals motivated me to keep setting new goals and working toward them until I accomplished them. I would go around to houses that had high grass and offer to cut it for a low price, if they had a lawnmower that I could use. Very quickly, I had a nice number of yards that I cut continuously. By 12, I had saved up enough money to buy a car. It was a 1972 Gremlin. I loved my car. One of my older friends Louis, taught me to drive. I was the only person in Junior high that could drive myself to school. I became an instant celebrity because I could give friends a ride to and from the skating rink for a small price. Even in school this goal-oriented mindset helped me stick with tasks I did not like to do, such as reading, science, math, and just sitting in class.

Setting and achieving goals are crucial to success. Envision what you want and write it down. Studies state that written goals have more influence over our actions. Now set up your action plan to accomplish your goal. Next break it down into achievable steps. Understand that Rome was not built in a day. Having patience, persistence and work ethic is the foundation of your blueprint.

Patience will allow you to be able to mentally accept when things don't go as planned. Failure does not mean give up. Every failure brings you closer to success if you have the patience to stay committed to your goal. Think of it this way when something that you have attempted one way does not work, then you know to try a different way. We learn from our past mistakes and we grow from the acquired knowledge.

Persistence is the attitude that you will succeed by any means necessary. If you are knocked down eight times, then you get up nine times. I can recall when I was first learning how to dunk a basketball. I'm sure that I failed at least 1000 times a week. I never stopped and even at age 44 today, I can walk in any gym and dunk a basketball.

Your work ethic is the heart of your success. Without it nothing works. Just as if your heart stopped right now, your body would shut down almost immediately. Keep your heart (work ethic) strong by utilizing it frequently, and positively in all things that you do.

Surround yourself with positive people who have goals that are in line with your own. Listen and learn from people who have accomplished what you are working toward. Make sure your goals line up with your values and don't allow anyone to sway are deter your desires.

Certain things I know about money to be true. Money can't stop death or buy back your health. While pursuing your goals don't forget that there are people and other things more important than money. For me, my kids are my top priority and even if I would not have had the injuries that benched me from professional basketball once my son was born, I would not have allowed playing to interfere with my parenting.

Make sure that as you are working on accomplishing your goals that you are helping and assisting people with there's as well. You will be amazed how much helping other people helps you become successful. Below are a few key concepts to assist with goal setting.

1. **Building financial success requires a Blueprint and takes patience.** Nothing great is achieved without a plan, and unless you hit the lottery it takes time to execute and achieve your goals.

2. **Envision what standard of living you desire.** Start to work on your vision immediately. First steps are by saving, budgeting, and working hard to earn money.

3. **Live beneath your means.** It is ok not to have the newest phone or pair of shoes simply because you have the money or means to purchase it. Look around your room and your closet how much money would you have saved if you chose less expensive things or did not purchase items that you didn't need?

4. **Create a budget for daily, weekly, and monthly spending.** This will keep you on tract an organized with your finances. This is also great practice for when you have your own business or a position running someone else business.

5. **Always have a built-in financial cushion.** You want to always be prepared for life when it throws you financial curve balls.

6. **Acquire different money-making skill sets**. The more skills and education you have, the more marketable you will be.

7. **There is no wrong time to learn to manage money.** I like to use the age range 8 to 80. No matter your age or financial status your financial responsibility depends on your ability to manage money.

8. **Surround yourself with people who manage money**. This may seem obvious, but who you hang around with has an influence on you. Remember, you are the average of the four people with whom you spend the most time.

9. **Set a budget and adhere to it.** The only way to accomplish your financial goals is that you are disciplined enough to stick to it.

Credit Wise

Diminishing Debt, Replenishes U

When I first started investing in real estate, I used cash advance convenience checks from credit cards to purchase property. This would typically be high risk, but because they were 0 percent interest for the life of the balance, the risk factor was depleted to almost nothing. I've learned the ins and outs of how to use your credit wisely. Credit can be a great source of capital if you get the right interest rate. Using money to make more money is much better when you can use borrowed money at little to know interest. Using credit cards can also build your credit score when used properly. Look for credit cards that give cash back rewards for making purchases. A rewards system is a way of making money instead of paying interest on the carryover amount month to month. Use a card with a low-interest rate in case you get into a bind and cannot pay off the balance monthly. I have found that credit unions have the best interest rates on credit cards. Of course, everything credits wise considers your credit score.

Often I'm asked when a good time is to apply for credit. My answer is only apply for cards or loans when your credit score is 680 or higher. You can build your score by periodically using credit cards and paying them off. Make sure you are making on time payments for any and all loans that you have including student loans. If you cannot get a credit card because your score is too low, then I suggest getting a secured credit card. This type of card is secured by an account with a certain amount of money in it that is equal to or more than the credit limit. When it comes time to make a big purchase, lenders see that you have a history of good money-making decisions and that you pay back what you borrow. You can also negotiate interest rate, membership fees, even balances with credit card companies. Monitor your credit score and keep it in good standing. The credit bureaus consider any score over 680 to be a "good" credit score. Once a year you are allowed one free credit report from all three credit bureaus.

If you are a parent, start your children's credit history off early by giving them a card with a meager limit, such as $200. Allow them to learn to budget and pay off their card each month with your help, if that's feasible. Also, warn them that many credit card companies prey on unsuspecting college students by giving them high credit limits and enticing them to go into debt.

Bad credit affects your interest rates. Interest rate is what determines your payback amount. This affects all major purchases that you borrow money for, such as a house, car, furniture and anything that requires you to borrow money. Now a days your credit score even affects how much you pay for insurance. I recently learned that even some utility companies use your credit score to determine if you must pay a deposit for services. A low credit score can even prevent you from getting certain jobs. Thus, it is vital that you make a point to use good judgement when you are applying for credit or getting a loan.

Bad credit can be repaired with discipline and a strategic actionable plan (blueprint). Make it a habit not to spend what you can't pay off by the end of the month. You want to maintain a good impression for lenders to be able to establish yourself well in life. Using credit cards wisely comes down to you being discipline and logical with spending. If you have a pattern of making bad choices with credit, then I suggest that you only allow yourself one card with a very small balance on it. Stop the interest accumulation on any other credit cards that you hold by calling the credit card companies and working out payment plans. If you have some cash you can negotiate settlements that are pennies on the dollar. If you are not comfortable negotiating settlements then reach out to a credit repair company.

It only took me one time to create a lot of credit card debt to realize that it is not worth all the high interest, and extra money you pay for that money. I made that mistake after my divorce. Soon as I moved back into my house, I made several purchases driven purely by emotions. I went and bought all new furniture, appliances, and bedroom sets. It took me a weekend to create the debt and a few years to pay it off.

Adhere to these simple steps, and you can enjoy all the benefits that using credit cards have to offer.

1. **Don't spend money on credit cards that you cannot afford to pay off monthly.** Sometimes emergencies happen but make it a priority to payoff credit card balances as soon as possible. If you get overwhelmed are in too much debt then you can afford do not be ashamed to start over.

2. **Leave your credit cards at home if tempted to impulsive buying.** This has saved me and my kids plenty of times. I even travel with one credit card that only has my trip budgeted amount as the limit.

3. **Limit eating out.** If you pay close attention to what you are spending on and notice that a significant amount is going toward eating out, stop it.

4. **Cancel any reoccurring subscriptions that you no longer use.** I notice that I had reoccurring payments on all my vehicles to carwashes during the wintertime. It was a total waste of money.

5. **Unsubscribe to store emails.** Stop the temptations, I truly believe the saying (out of site out of mind).

6. **Look for sales ads for items you intend on purchasing.** You will be amazed at how many things have coupons online or in your local paper.

7. **Do not accept high interests credit cards, or ones with annual fees.** Apply for cards that have cash-back options or if you like to travel, get one that allows your purchases to earn frequent flyer miles.

How To Make Money

Making Money Is a choice

At age 24, a couple of back and ankle injuries shattered my professional basketball career. On top of that, I was newly married, with a son on the way. It was time for me to figure out the next chapter of life. My wife and mother in-law influenced (strongly forced) me to move back to St. Louis. The new challenge was figuring out what to do with my life, since basketball was no longer an option. I had not thought about it. How was I going to make money? First, I was optimistic because I had my college degree. I applied to many places and never secured a position. Starting to feel discouraged, I humbled myself and decided to go to a temp agency. All the positions at the agency were clerical in nature. I was like no way. A few bills later, I accepted an assignment at some large insurance firm as a secretary. Although this was incredibly humbling to go from the professional athlete to secretary, I understood that I had to do whatever it took to take care of my family. Every day I was suited and booted and would arrive 15 minutes early to work. I also made it a point to be very productive as well as friendly to everyone in the building. By the third day, the owner of the company noticed me and asked me to have a seat in his office. Richard asked me why I was working through a staffing agency. I explained my situation to him, and then he asked me where I would like to be working. I told him I enjoyed working with kids. I told him that I am job hunting for nonprofit organizations. He told me that he has a contact at a place that would be perfect for me. It was The Boy Scouts of America. He got me an interview, and I was hired within the week. Working for The Boy Scouts was a great job that paid a lot more money than the temp agency and gave me flexible hours.

Although I made enough to take care of my family's basic needs, I was not comfortable. I desired to make more. I went back into thinking mode to figure out how I could grow my money and make it work for me. I started researching a lot of different money-making opportunities, and the most interesting was real estate. Because of my upbringing, I felt it very important to keep a roof over my family head and plan for a future that made sure that my kids were always taken care of. My wife and I were young and could not work out our differences, so it led us to divorce. The dissolution of our marriage was expensive and mentally draining, but I learned a crucial lesson from it. I learned to always have a financial plan B for life's unexpected expenses.

Every failure is a doorway to a new accomplishment. During the divorce, I had to buy my ex-wife out of the house. This allowed me to learn a little about real estate. I learned about home equity, debt ratio, and cash out refinancing. I needed to make more money, so I started job hunting for a second side job. The first option for me was to do something working with kids. So, I started substitute teaching. I loved substituting, so I pursued proper credentials to become a teacher.

Turn lemons into Lemonade. It was from my divorce; my real estate life was born. Now that real estate had my attention I wanted to learn everything that I could about investing. What transpired next I could have never imagined. Short version is that I have been able to buy anything and everything that I ever dreamed of and make the type of money that I only thought possible by being a professional athlete or entertainer.

In my opinion Real estate is the easiest way to make money. In order to get started all you need to do is save a little cash are have great credit. There are even ways around credit concerns. Most banks want your credit score to be 680 are better and they want you to have 20 to 25 percent to put down. They also want the property to be livable. Those terms and deals may be a little harder to achieve, but not impossible. The other option is hard money lenders. These lenders don't require credit in most cases and will lend on any home of value if the numbers work out. The numbers typically must be less then 75 percent of the home value once rehabbed. These types of loans have higher interest rates but are ideal for fix and flip projects or fix up, refinance and rent projects.

They typically only require 10 percent down. There is a great company that I had great success with called Long Horn Investments. This company lends the money to buy the property and to rehab it.

Think about this scenario, you find a home that is for sale for 50 thousand and it needs 20 thousand to update to sale. After fixing it up it is worth 100 thousand. Let's say you use a company like Long Horn as your lender. They will lend you all the money to complete the project with as little as 10 percent coming out of your own pocket. Do the math-once the home sells then you profited a pretty penny. Reinvest your profits into more projects. Now imagine doing 4 projects like that a year and instantly you have a six-figure income.

Here are a few best practice suggestions about making money.

1. Have a plan for the money that you make. First part of the plan starts with saving. Try to save at least 20 percent of your monthly income. It's amazing how things come together with proper planning, the same is true for your financial future. A plan allows you to know how much you need to make to reach your goals.

2. Develop a budget that incorporates money that you plan on investing. My suggestion is a minimum of 20

percent of your income should be invested in some sort of business are investment.

3. With work, you can rectify any financial problems and achieve any financial goals. Everyone that grew up with me as a kid could never imagine I would grow up and achieve the things that I have been able to with hard work.

4. The sooner you start financial planning the better. There is no right or wrong age to start or restart your financial plan. I have all my kids work on their financial future by saving 50 percent of all the money that they earn or receive in gifts. I invested their college fund in real estate so not only does the rental homes cash flow, but also builds equity over time. Also, while in college, the money that they receive from their rental home, I urged them to invest in stocks.

5. When financing a home or automobile, plan your budget using the shortest-term loan allowable. For instance, all my financed homes are on 15-year mortgages, and my car loans are 36 months. This will save you a lot of money on interest and money saved is just like money earned.

6. Make your 24-hour day count. Understand that time is money. Make sure you are applying majority of your time to reaching your goals. There have been times that I have worked 20-hour days doing

4 different jobs to accomplish financial goals or pay some bills.

Put your MONEY to WORK for you

If you do not make your money work for you, then you will spend your entire life working for your money.

It was a new beginning. After going through the refinance process of the house, I decided to give real estate a chance. I started researching different methods on how to become a real estate investor. I found that the most helpful, resourceful, and knowledgeable people were real estate agents. So, I went to Real Estate school to get my license.

The two most critical ingredients to real estate investing are good credit and capital. I had good credit but very little money. So, I used 0 interest cash advance convenience checks from my credit cards to finance my first investment property. I bought a house on the south side of St. Louis for 20 thousand dollars. It had a lot of potential, but needed a lot of work. I did not have the funds to hire rehab contractors, so I did most of the work on it myself. It took me six months and I sold it for 45 thousand. After materials and other cost associated with the rehab, I made a net profit of 20 thousand in just six months. I paid down half of my credit card debt and re-invested the balance into another flip project. Within the next twelve months, I made double my work salary.

Flipping was going pretty well, but it was tough to keep good contractors. The more work I gave them, the more money they wanted. The payouts from flipping houses was lucrative, but far and few between. I had to figure out a way to bring more money in more often, so I decided to start renting. Becoming a landlord was the perfect answer. I could buy two units at a time, and while waiting on one project to be completed, the other one could be rented. Now I had properties in cash flowing for me. Renting turned out to be very lucrative. Not only did it save me from having to pay utilities, but it also increased my cash flow and net profits. Now with more cash flow, I could buy more units and make more money.

Over the next four years, I purchased a lot of units and built a solid real estate portfolio. I no longer needed to work a 9 to 5 job. I built my dream home, a 7500 square foot mansion equipped with seven bedrooms, ten bathrooms, eight-car garage, indoor pool, and every amenity that I had ever fantasied. I also bought every car that I ever wanted to fill each garage. I traveled places I had always dreamed of going. I helped my friends and family get houses and also taught them how to invest. I was not even 30 years old, and I had achieved every financial goal I set for myself.

Although real estate has been my most lucrative way of making my money work for me, I've also invested in stocks and other business. I also max out my 401K.

Investing in stocks has also been a way for me to make my money work for me. My first experience with money working for me was through the stock market in college. The stock market can be quite lucrative, but make sure you educate yourself and hire a trusted financial advisor starting out. The next step is to open an account then familiarize yourself with the different stocks. Set a budget for how much you want to invest and then start investing. Be aggressive and don't be afraid to take risk. Only invest money that you can comfortably afford to lose. If your job matches what you contribute to your retirement fund max that amount out. Next, think about retirement and invest in annuities to secure your financial future. You don't want to outlive your financial resources and while living, you want to do so comfortably.

After my mother passed, I thought seriously about the financial future of my family. I wanted to secure my children's future, so I invested in a life insurance policy. Don't think Life insurance policies just for death benefits think of them as stability, and a financial future for your legacy. Although I raise my kids to be independent and self-sufficient, when I pass I want to still be able to assist.

The way my financial mindset is set up the purpose of money is for it to make more money. There are so many ways to make money today that all you must decide is which one, are which one's you want to pursue. Below are a few suggestions:

Figure out strategies to make extra money. This can be driving Uber, Lyft, Door dash, cutting grass, painting or anything that you don't mind doing that pays you.

Create Residual income. There is nothing more exciting then financial freedom. When you stay within your income limits you can enjoy life more.

Once you have built up your savings with 6 months reserve, start looking to buy a rental house. Rental income in my opinion is the best cash flowing investment you can make. Imagine buying two rental houses a year that make an extra $500 a month each. In ten years, you will have an extra 10 thousand a month coming in. Not to mention how much the homes will have appreciated.

FINANCIAL SUCCESS BLUEPRINT

Quality decision making is the key to a financial success. Everything is an extension of your actions, so having an actionable game plan will set you up for the goals you desire. If you can visualize the objective, you can achieve it. Decide where you want to see yourself in the future? Start with a vision and then write it down. Break your goal down into doable steps. Come up with a realistic time frame for the completion of each step. Consistently achieving small goals will eventually lead you to your ultimate large ones.

Financial Success has many definitions. Popular opinion of success suggest that you must make a million a year to be considered successful. Under that ideology less than 0.09% of all people are successful. This viewpoint is extremely outdated. Everyone's success picture is different. The most important, accurate definition is the one that you create for yourself. This explanation of accomplishment should be motivated by your desires, dreams, and goals. There is no one number that makes up your financial significance. It's a continues process of setting monetary goals and accomplishing them. Some standard goals should be your baseline. Here is a recap of some of the things that you need to work towards.

1. Always have 6 months reserve in your savings account. If you are just starting out work toward 3 months reserve before you start to invest.

2. Always save 20 percent of your monthly income.

3. Make a habit of making good financial decisions. This is important to practice all the time. Going out to eat, purchasing new shoes or cloths, buying a car or house all money decisions should be calculated and logically decided.

4. Establish A financial blueprint. Your blueprint is your working actionable plan to achieve. The objective of a financial blueprint is to build security through earning, savings and investing.

5. To build wealth make your money work for you. I can not stress this point enough look to acquire real estate.

6. No one else definition or number makes up your economic success or significance. Come up with the amount you need to live the life that you desire.

7. Understand that your financial blueprint is a continuous process of setting monetary goals and accomplishing them.

8. Proper Money Management is the Secret to Stability.

9. Have a money mindset. This is an attitude that you have about your finances. It's the driving force for making decisions about your money. Having the right attitude about finances will help you avoid and overcome challenges.

10. Understand with work that any financial difficulty can be rectified. The secret is to live within your means and don't accumulate debt. Keep a financial planner and track your ins and outs, so you know where you stand at any moment.

11. Invest in yourself and your future. College degrees, certifications, licenses, and specific job training are all good investments to better yourself and create more money-making opportunities. Getting a higher education is statistically proven to increase income potential.

12. Surround yourself with people who manage money well and have a positive money mindset. Remember, you are the average of the five people with whom you spend the most time.

13. Read, Research, and Reflect. Educate yourself on money management. Learn about different investments. Think about what you learned and make it benefit you.

14. Get a mentor. Find someone who is doing what you want to do are living how you want to live and ask them to mentor you.

15. Post daily affirmations that reflect what you want financially. Spoken words become a reality.

16. Your money should make more money. There are many ways to make your money work for you. Best practice is to use a combination of strategies with different investments to achieve your financial goals. Figure out Strategies and investment that allow your money to work for you.

17. Make sure to keep your savings in an account that pays you interest. 18.Find ways to make passive income. Passive income earned with little to no effort, but this requires an upfront investment.

18. Start saving for retirement immediately. Retirement accounts such as 401(k)s and I.R.A.s are investment accounts. They invest and make money for you.

19. Consider silently partnering in a business. Be sure to do your homework.

20. Real Estate is always an excellent choice to not only build wealth, but also a legacy for generations to come. You can invest in fixing up and sell or to become a landlord and rent out properties. Either

way, there is an excellent potential to increase your cash flow.

Conclusion

True success is a succession of good quality decisions that lead to a life you love. Children as well as adults need to know that hard work is not in vain and there is a better way of life. Just don't quit dreaming and don't stop working hard in pursuit of your dreams and goals. With a dream, a blueprint, action and courage, you can achieve anything your heart desires.

True success is a process of life lessons and accrued wisdom resulting in a life that makes you healthy, wealthy, and wise on your terms. Reflecting on these impoverished times, I think of how things could have been a lot worse. There is always a scenario that could be worse. Next, I focus on all the skills I acquired during this stage of my childhood. I learned people would pay for convenience. I also realized that no matter what profession you decide to pursue, you must put time, effort, and energy into it. I promised myself that I would always be in financial position to not have to work for anyone. Number 1 reason is for my kids. My main focal point is to never have to miss a school event, sporting event, or anything important that my babies want me to attend.

Everything in life that I enjoy doing, I figured out how to make it make me money. Some required me to earn degrees and certifications. These goals required a lot of time and a lot of test-taking. I am not a fan of test-taking, and I never enjoyed sitting in college classes being lectured. Although no one in my family before me graduated from college, I understood the importance of education. I learned that nothing worthwhile comes easy, but the willingness to push yourself to accomplish goals will align you with your wants and needs in life.

To date, I have earned an associate degree in business and my bachelor's degree in criminal justice. I hold two master's degrees one in teaching and one in education. I earned an elementary teaching certification in 1-6 grade. I completed massage school and a fitness certification. I'm a licensed real estate agent and investor. I am part owner and investor of multiple businesses; I have a massive real estate portfolio. I'm also a sixth grade Math and Science teacher. I teach because I LOVE IT, and I feel it is extremely critical that we start mentoring, modeling, and teaching our youth how to overcome adversity and be successful. Although I have employees I pay larger salaries than mine from teaching, it makes me feel good to be able to do what I genuinely love and allots me the opportunity to mentor, motivate and teach at risk youth. Through my journey, I have had the chance to get to know and learn from some of the top C.E.O.'s, educators, and entrepreneurs in business today. I have also trained and studied with some of the top fitness professionals. I'm sharing and passing the knowledge I have gained through experience, failures, successes, and research. All my life experiences rather good, bad, or ugly, have assisted me in achieving True Success.